HANDS-ON SCIENCE

GAMES, PUZZLES, AND TOYS

Step-by-Step Science Activity Projects
from the Smithsonian Institution

Gareth Stevens Publishing
MILWAUKEE

For a free color catalog describing Gareth Stevens' list of high-quality books, call 1-800-542-2595 (USA) or 1-800-461-9120 (Canada). Gareth Stevens' Fax: (414) 225-0377.

Library of Congress Cataloging-in-Publication Data

Hands-on science: games, puzzles, and toys / by Megan Stine . . . [et al.] ; illustrated by Simms Taback.
     p. cm. -- (Hands-on science, step-by-step science activity projects from the Smithsonian Institution)
     Series originally published by the Smithsonian Institution as a series of science activity calendars.
     Includes bibliographical references and index.
     ISBN 0-8368-0957-2
     1. Science--Experiments--Juvenile literature. 2. Scientific recreations--Juvenile literature. 3. Sports--Experiments--Juvenile literature. I. Stine, Megan. II. Taback, Simms, ill. III. Series: Hands-on science (Milwaukee, Wis.).
Q164.H247 1993
507.8--dc20   92-56892

Produced and published by
Gareth Stevens Publishing
1555 North RiverCenter Drive, Suite 201
Milwaukee, Wisconsin 53212, USA

Series editor: Patricia Lantier-Sampon
Book designer: Sabine Beaupré
Editorial assistants: Jamie Daniel and Diane Laska

Printed in the United States of America

2 3 4 5 6 7 8 9 99 98 97 96 95 94

CONTENTS

Weights and Measures Abbreviation Key

U.S. Units

in = inch	oz = ounce	
ft = foot	qt = quart	
tsp = teaspoon	gal = gallon	
T = tablespoon	lb = pound	
C = cup	°F = °Fahrenheit	

Metric Units

cm = centimeter	kg = kilogram
m = meter	km = kilometer
ml = milliliter	°C = °Centigrade
l = liter	
g = gram	

INTRODUCTION

By the 21st century, our society will demand that all its citizens possess basic competencies in the fundamentals of science and technology. As science becomes the dominant subject of the workplace, it is important to equip children with an understanding and appreciation of science early in their lives.

Learning can, and does, occur in many places and many situations. Learning occurs in school, at home, and on the trip between home and school. This book provides suggestions for interactive science activities that can be done in a variety of settings, using inexpensive and readily available materials. The experiments, activities, crafts, and games included in this book allow you, whether teacher or parent, to learn science along with the children.

SOME SUGGESTIONS FOR TEACHERS

The activities in this book should be used as supplements to your normal classroom science curricula. Since they were originally developed for use in out-of-school situations, they may require some minor modifications to permit a larger number of children to participate. Nonetheless, you will find that these activities lend themselves to a fun-filled science lesson for all participants.

SOME SUGGESTIONS FOR PARENTS

One of the most important jobs you have as a parent is the education of your children. Every day is filled with opportunities for you to actively participate in your child's learning. Through the **Hands-On Science** projects, you can explore the natural world together and make connections between classroom lessons and real-life situations.

FOR BOTH TEACHERS AND PARENTS

The best things you can bring to each activity are your experience, your interest, and, most importantly, your enthusiasm. These materials were designed to be both educational and enjoyable. They offer opportunities for discovery, creative thinking, and fun.

HOW TO USE THIS BOOK

There are ten activities in this book. Since every classroom and family is different, not all activities will be equally suitable. Browse through the book and find the ones that seem to make sense for your class or family. There is no prescribed order to these activities, nor any necessity to do all of them.

At the beginning of each activity is a list of all the materials you will need to do the project. Try to assemble all of these items before you begin. The procedures have been laid out in an easy-to-follow, step-by-step guide. If you follow these directions, you should have no difficulty doing the activity. Once you have completed the basic activity, there are also suggested variations that you can try now, or later. At the end of each activity is an "Afterwords" section to provide additional information.

BUBBLE BREW

BUBBLE BREW

Who doesn't like bubbles? Bubbles can be very scientific, but best of all they are fun to make and watch, which should take about 45 minutes.

YOU WILL NEED

Some thick liquid dishwashing detergent (Joy works well)
Newspaper
Measuring cup
Flat plate or tray
Soda straws
2 or 3 Empty tin cans of the same size
Can opener
Masking tape
Styrofoam or paper cups (1 per person)
Wire coat hanger
Paper clips, ruler, tap water
Heavy cotton cord or string, 3 feet long
Karo syrup, Jell-O powder, Certo, salad oil, or food coloring (optional)

1 To concoct your Bubble Brew, put six ounces of water in a cup and add one ounce of dishwashing liquid. Any time you want to make up some Bubble Brew, use six measures of water to one measure of detergent. Add the detergent to the water and stir gently.

2 Get ready to bubble! Bubbles are fun, but they can get messy. If you are working indoors, take some newspaper and cover the floor and tables so they won't get wet. You can work outside if there isn't too much breeze.

3 Try blowing half-bubbles. Smear some Bubble Brew on a flat plate or tray (or the tabletop, if your parents don't mind it getting wet). Dip one end of a soda straw in the Brew and hold it just above the wet table or plate. Blow gently into your straw. How large a bubble can you make? What happens when you touch a bubble with a wet straw? A dry one?

4 Try blowing another bubble *inside* your first one. Keep your straw wet. How many bubbles can you blow inside each other?

Make a small bubble right beside a bigger one. Let them touch. Which bubble bulges into the other? Is it always the same-size bubble? Blow several bubbles and look for a place where four walls meet. Build some bubble houses and towns. **If all this blowing makes you feel dizzy, take a break!**

5 Big Bubbles! Use a can opener to cut the ends out of two or three tin cans, then tape them together. Tape some plastic soda straws across the joints to make your tin-can tube stronger. If it's okay with your folks, wet the whole tabletop with Brew. Dip one end of your tin-can tube in the Brew. Make sure the Brew forms a window over the end when you take it out. Blow gently through the cans, with-

USE SAME SIZE CANS—OPEN AT ALL ENDS

TAPE OVER STRAWS & JOINTS

out touching your lips to the cut metal. How big a bubble can you blow on the table? Get a friend to help you. Look at your images in the bubble.

6 Floaters! Stand away from the table. Blow as big a bubble as you can out of the end of your tin-can tube. Gently raise your tube and twist it at the same time. Practice until you can cut off the bubble. Try making bubbles by blowing through a pencil hole in the bottom of a Styrofoam or paper cup, after dipping the open end in Brew.

7 Super-Big Bubbles (Lucky Loops) Make up enough Bubble Brew to almost fill a large tray. Run about three feet of heavy cotton cord or string through two milkshake straws. Knot the cord and move the knot inside one of the straws. Put your Lucky Loop into the tray of Brew. Get it all wet— your fingers, too! Hold onto the straws and slowly lift your Lucky Loop out of the Brew.

2 PAPER CLIPS → ← STRAWS →

Practice moving your loop through the air to make *super-big* bubbles! Walk quickly and see how long a bubble you can make. Twist the two straws toward one another to cut off a bubble. Practice! Practice! Practice!

Try the same thing with a loop made from a coat hanger. Hold one finger at the bottom of the hook. Remember, keep everything wet with Brew, including your finger.

8 Other Bubble Makers
You can make bubbles with anything that has a hole right through it. Try using a funnel, a piece of hose or plastic pipe, a piece of window screen, a cardboard roll from wax paper or foil, or whatever else you can find.

9 Bubbles That Aren't Round?
Cut some soda straws into pieces about 3 inches long. Clip two paper clips together and stick each free end into a separate piece of straw. Use more straws and clips to build structures like these. Get

some wire you can twist into different shapes.

What shape of bubble can you make with these? What does your image look like in these "windows"? Dip each one into the Brew. Get it all wet. Let windows form in all spaces. What happens if windows happen to touch? Break one window at a time with a dry straw.

VARIATIONS

■ Experiment with making stronger bubbles. Try adding different amounts of Karo syrup, or Certo, or Jell-O powder to your Bubble Brew. Try adding some salad oil to your detergent before you mix it in the water.

■ Can you draw a map of something you cannot see? Release some bubbles outside and watch where they go. Now you can draw a map of air currents you cannot see.

■ What colors can you see in your bubbles? Where do they come from? What can you do to change the color of light hitting the bubbles? The color of the solution? Try using colored cellophane and food coloring to find out.

■ How long can you keep one bubble? What can you do

to protect it? Set up a contest with rules. Do bubbles shrink in the refrigerator?

■ How high can you make a half-bubble? How wide? Use a wet ruler to find out.

AFTERWORDS

Liquids are made up of small particles called *molecules*. You can't see them, not even with a microscope. There is a layer of molecules at the surface of a liquid, hooked together just like links in a chain. Now think of when you pull on a string or a chain. You are putting *tension* on it. The chain of molecules in a liquid is also under a kind of tension, called *surface tension*.

If you want to see the effect of surface tension, try this: Dip one end of a dry soda straw into plain water. Hold it upright and see how much water is left in the straw. It doesn't all run out! Next add a few drops of detergent to the water and try again. How much of this solution runs out the bottom of the straw? You'll find that the detergent lowers the surface tension of the water and the solution flows more easily than plain water.

Adding detergent to water also makes it easier to blow bubbles. See the differ-

ence it makes if you use rain water to make Bubble Brew instead of tap water. Rain water has lower surface tension than most tap water.

You may have noticed that it was difficult to make a square bubble by blowing through a tube. Even if you used a square wire frame, you won't get square bubbles. Liquids tend to form drops in the shape of balls, or *spheres*. The *energy* in the surface layer of molecules is trying to make things easy for itself. The best shape for holding the most liquid within the smallest surface is a sphere. What shapes do water droplets form on the waxed surface of a car?

Did you notice that whenever four bubble walls come together, one of them usually breaks? That's because three walls coming together are more stable, or steady, than four. For instance, you may have seen lots of four-legged tables that wobbled. But have you ever seen a wobbly three-legged table? Probably not.

Whenever you make a bubble next to another bubble of a different size, the wall of the smaller bubble always bulges into the space of the larger bubble. In other words,

the smaller bubble always wins the shoving match. You see, the *pressure* inside smaller bubbles is greater than the pressure inside larger bubbles. Remember how hard it is to blow up a balloon at first? But the bigger the balloon gets, the easier it is to keep blowing it up. Pressure is the *force* (push or pull) on a surface. The same force (your breath) is spread over a larger surface area in a bigger bubble than in a smaller one. That is why the smaller bubble has greater pressure.

Did you see all of the colors of the rainbow in your bubbles? These colors are contained in sunlight. You saw the *visible spectrum* of white (seen) light: red, orange, yellow, green, blue, violet. You usually can't see the separate colors in sunlight. You need water droplets (rain) or a thin film (soap bubble) to sort them out. The business of sorting out the separate colors of the spectrum is called *dispersion*. Oil on a puddle will also disperse the rainbow colors in the visible spectrum. Where else have you seen these colors? Maybe you'll find a pot of gold at the end of *your* rainbow!

ROCKETS AWAY

ROCKETS AWAY

Do you have dreams of being an astronaut? First you have to learn how to get your rocketship off the ground. You'll be airborne in only 30 minutes!

YOU WILL NEED

A plastic tennis-ball can or
    plastic soda bottle
    with cap
Large nail or pencil
Scissors
Soda straws of 3 different
    types: jumbo, super
    jumbo, and flexible
    (see **Note**)
Tape
Paper
Several small pieces of
    hook tape
A "woolly" blanket
A plastic bag, about
    10" by 12"
Some fishing line,
    6- or 8-pound test
A few balloons, *long* rather
    than round
Vinegar
Baking soda

Note: Most large drinking straws — the kind you get at burger joints — are *jumbo* straws. However, a few fast-food places (like Burger King or ice-cream parlors that serve thick milk shakes) have even larger straws — *super jumbo*. For this activity you will need a few of each and the jumbo should be able to pass smoothly *through* the super jumbo. You might also want to get some *flexible* straws (ones that have a bend like an accordion partway down the straw); they're available at the supermarket.

You can use air power to learn some rules that are important for understanding flight and trajectory (the path your rocketship will take in space). Get set to make your own rockets and a launcher!

1 Poke a hole in the lid of the plastic tennis-ball can with a large nail or pencil. If using a soda bottle, you might have to use a drill to make a hole in the cap. Or try using the pointed end of a pair of scissors. (Ask a grown-up for help if you need it.)

2 Cut the end of the flex straw on an angle and run it through the hole in the lid or cap. The straw should fit very snug. Put the lid or cap back on the can or bottle.

3 Stick a *jumbo* straw into the end of the flex straw and tape it in place. The flex straw will allow you to adjust the angle of launch during later experiments. Your rocket launcher is now complete!

POKE HOLE IN LID
CUT ANGLE
TAPE JUMBO TO FLEXIBLE STRAW
PLASTIC TENNIS BALL CAN

4 Now, make some rockets. Fold over 1/8" of the end of a *super jumbo* straw and tape it down. Slide the super jumbo over the jumbo launcher straw, aim, and give the can or bottle a sharp squeeze. The super jumbo should take off! Practice launches to see if you can land your rocket in a box or wastebasket. Try it from different locations around the room. Then put some obstacles in its path to see if you can get your rocket high enough to sail over them.

VARIATIONS

■ *Stabilizers* are often attached to flying devices to help them fly straight. Find out how various stabilizer designs help or hinder the straight flight of your rockets. Tape on paper fins (2, 3, or 4), cones, or other designs.

■ Does a short rocket fly farther than a long one? Make different rockets (2", 4", and 6" long), fit them all with identical stabilizers, and find out which flies best.

■ A target makes all of the experiments more interesting! Get a bit of *hook Velcro* and tape it to the front tip of your rockets. Search around the house for a blanket that the

Velcro-tipped rocket will easily stick to. Hang the blanket over a door. Now launch the rocket and try to stick it to the blanket. How high can you stick a rocket? What is the greatest distance from which you can stick the rocket to the blanket?

■ Make a Beeline Rocket Message Delivery System. Tape the soda straw to the side seam of a plastic bag. Run a length of fishing line through the straw long enough to tie one end of the line to something in one room, and the other end of the line to something in another room. Write a message and put it in the bag. The open end of the

ZOOM!

GIVE PLASTIC CAN A SHARP SQUEEZE!

PUT BALLOON INTO BAG WITH MESSAGE

STRAWS

FISHING LINE

TAPE SODA STRAW TO PLASTIC BAG

TAPE A BIT OF HOOK VELCRO TO END OF ROCKET

HANG BLANKET OVER DOOR OR TALL CHAIR

bag should face *away* from where you want your message to go. Blow up a balloon and pinch the opening shut, put it into the bag with the message, and release it. Your message will rocket into the next room!

■ Real rockets don't run on air, of course. They use fuel that burns, or *combusts,* and the power sends them off into space. You can make your own rocket fuel. Pour 1 cup of vinegar into the can or bottle. Then take 2 tablespoons of baking soda, roll it up into a paper napkin, and insert it in the can or bottle. Replace the lid or cap and swirl the container to mix the ingredients together. Zoom!

AFTERWORDS

Real rockets don't fly on compressed air power. Real rockets have *internal combustion engines* and carry both fuel to burn and a source of oxygen to help the combustion. Because rockets carry their own oxygen source, they can operate even in the deep reaches of space where very little air exists.

Rocket propulsion works because of a very basic law of physics: For every action, there is an equal, and oppo-

site, reaction. Fuel is burned in a closed chamber. The hot gases that result from the combustion rush out the nozzle at great speed. The fast-moving gases that are propelled out the end of the rocket are the "action." The opposite "reaction" moves the rocket forward. This simple principle drives rockets to the moon and beyond!

Your soda-straw rocket carries no fuel for propulsion; the driving force behind the rocket is air pressure. When you squeeze the flexible plastic bottle, the air in the bottle is compressed into a smaller space and the pressure inside increases. The air pushes out in all directions with equal force. When the increased force pushes against the closed end of the rocket straw, the force is strong enough to send the rocket off into space.

If the force is applied for a short time, the rocket will move slower. The longer the force acts on the rocket, the faster the rocket will be going when it leaves the launcher.

This fact suggests that a longer straw rocket will fly faster (therefore farther) than a short one. Did you figure that out yourself?

For a brief moment during the launch of a soda-straw rocket, it acts like a real rocket. Precisely when the rocket leaves the launcher and the pressure inside the straw is vented through the open end of the straw, it acts just like a full-fledged rocket. For a split second, air will rush out the open end of the straw as it leaves the launcher. This action will have the *reaction* of adding a little thrust to the straw rocket. The effect will be small, but nonetheless the thrust will help the rocket move. The rest of the rocket's flight can be attributed to the push given to the rocket by the action of compressed air.

Another force to be dealt with in rocketry is air. Air is like a fluid; it has mass and occupies space. It must be pushed out of the way if an object is to pass through it. Therefore, the more streamlined you make your rocket, the more easily it will push through the air. Put this force to work *for* you. In order to keep the rocket on course, place stabi-

lizers, or fins, at the back of the rocket. As long as the rocket travels straight forward, the sharp edges of the fins cut efficiently through the air and keep the rocket steady. But if the rocket starts to pitch or roll, the broad side of the fin will start to make contact with the air, creating more air *resistance.* Increased resistance will tend to slow down that side of the rocket, which corrects the rocket's flight automatically. Now your rockets should make it safely to their destinations!

TOYING WITH SCIENCE

TOYING WITH SCIENCE

These science toys are so much fun you'll want to make them as gifts to give to your friends and family...after you've made your own to play with, of course! Each should take no more than 30 minutes to put together.

SKYHOOK

Can you balance your belt on your nose? Make cereal dance around? Create a tiny ocean, complete with waves, inside a bottle? Do these sound like some great feats of magic? Guess what? They're better than magic: They're scientific!

YOU WILL NEED

1 Wooden 12" ruler
1 Uncooked egg in its shell
Some modeling clay or dough
Felt-tip markers
Yarn scraps
1 Jackknife with a heavy
    handle (optional; to be
    used by adult)
Paper, pencil, scissors
2" by 4" Piece of wood,
    ³⁄₁₆" to ¼" wide
    (basswood or plywood)
Coping saw or scroll saw

1 Try to balance a ruler across the tip of one finger. You will probably find you can only do it if your finger is at the 6" mark or right in the middle of the ruler. The midpoint of that ruler is the center of gravity — where all the weight of an object is concentrated.

2 Now try balancing a raw egg on either end, in your hand. You will find that it's too hard to do: The base of the egg is too small and the center of gravity too high. But then tap the small end, making a hole about ¾" wide across the top. Empty the eggshell and wash it out well. Place a marble-sized piece of clay or dough into the eggshell so it sticks on the center of the bottom of the shell. Now balance the egg on its larger end. In fact, you probably can't even tip it over! You've lowered the center of gravity so far down that it is impossible to topple that egg.

STICK KNIFE ABOUT 1½" FROM BOTTOM

3 Let's get back to the ruler for a few minutes. Try balancing that same ruler upright on one fingertip. Almost impossible, isn't it? That's because the center of gravity is so high, the ruler becomes very unstable. Now ask an adult to open a jack-knife so the blade is at a right angle to its handle and stick the knife into the edge of the ruler at about 1½" from the bottom. That ruler will balance

THE SKYHOOK IS A GREAT GIFT!

LONG END OF SKYHOOK

BELT

on your fingertip! You have lowered the center of gravity so that it is below the ruler and in the knife and is now directly under your finger!

4 Now you're ready to make the skyhook: Trace the skyhook pattern onto thin paper and cut it out. Place the paper pattern on the wood and trace around pattern. With a coping or scroll saw, cut the wood along the line of the pattern. To use the skyhook, place a leather belt, at about the middle, into the skyhook's groove so both ends of the belt hang toward the longer part of the skyhook. Now hold the long end of the skyhook on the tip of your finger. It is amazingly stable! Place the long end of the skyhook on your nose. This "magical" toy makes a great gift!

STATIC CEREAL BOX

Have you ever walked across a carpeted room, reached for the metal door handle, and been zapped by an electrical shock that really tingled? Or have you ever rubbed a balloon on your sleeve and tried to stick it on a wall? You've been playing with electricity! This toy makes use of positive and negative electrical charges to amuse and amaze everyone.

YOU WILL NEED

Balloon
Salt, pepper
Plastic comb
Piece of nylon, fur, polyester, or wool (or wear clothes made of any of these materials)
Handful of puffed-rice or wheat cereal
1 Box with a clear plastic cover (the type that cards or stationery comes in works well)
Tape

1 If you haven't rubbed a balloon on your sleeve and stuck it to the wall, give it a try. Don't just watch what happens: Listen for the crackling sound made by the moving electric charges. If the room is dark enough, you might even see sparks.

2 Pour a little salt and pepper on a flat surface. Mix it up well. You will now be able to separate the pepper from the salt. Here's how: Rub the comb with nylon, wool, or fur (poly-

HOLD THE COMB 3/4" TO 1" ABOVE AND WATCH WHAT HAPPENS?

ester works well also). Hold the comb about 3/4" to 1" above the mixture and watch the pepper jump up to the comb. The salt will jump too, but not as high. You can easily remove the flakes of pepper from the salt mixture!

3 Now make the Static Cereal Box — a more permanent toy for playing with electrical charges. Put about 1/3 to 1/2 cup of cereal into the box. Place the clear plastic cover over it, and tape it down. Rub the box cover against you, if you are wearing something made of nylon, wool, fur, or polyester; or just rub the cover with a piece of one of these fabrics. Turn box so cover is up and watch the cereal cling to the top! If you place your finger on the cover, the cereal will dance around and shoot off the top. Have a race with someone else and see who can get one piece of cereal from one side of the cover to the other. Mark racing lines on the cover and give this toy as a present.

STORMY SEAS SODA BOTTLE

Did you ever shake up a bottle of oil-and-vinegar salad dressing and pour it over your salad — only to wind up with too much vinegar? Then you know that oil and water (or water-based vinegar) don't mix. You can pour them together, shake them vigorously, but eventually, they will go their separate ways.

YOU WILL NEED

Empty 1- or 2-liter colorless, plastic soda bottle with cap
Blue food coloring
Mineral oil (available in drugstores) or clear salad oil (you will probably need 1 pint of oil for the 1-liter bottle and 2 or 3 pints for the 2-liter bottle)
Scissors
Small scrap piece of white, bleach-bottle plastic

1 Pull off the plastic cup at the bottom of the soda bottle, if there is one, and save. Fill the bottle approximately half full of cool water. Add as many drops of food coloring as you desire to make the water a nice blue color. Mix well. Pour in the oil. If there is still space left in the bottle, add more oil or water until the bottle is filled right up to the neck.

OIL / COOL WATER AND COLORING / MINERAL OIL

2 With the scissors, cut out a tiny sailboat (or make several) from the scrap of bleach-bottle plastic. Insert the boat through the neck of the bottle. Watch what happens. It floats through the oil but stops before it gets to the blue water!

3 Close the cap very tightly. (You might want to place a small square of plastic wrap on top before replacing the cap.) Rock the bottle back and forth on its side. Watch the waves and bubbles form. To calm your seas, place the bottle back into its plastic bottom and let it set for a while. The oil and water will separate again — until your next storm at sea!

/ REMEMBER TO REPLACE CAP

AFTERWORDS

These science toys do indeed seem like magic tricks to anyone who doesn't understand the scientific principles behind them.

SKYHOOK

When you balance a ruler across one finger, you are demonstrating the center of gravity. In a regularly shaped object, the center of gravity is at the center of the object. An egg's center of gravity is near the center of the egg (on the inside) — yet because its base is too small, it is unable to balance itself. To balance an object, we can lower its center of gravity or widen its base.

In an irregularly shaped object, like your body, the center of gravity is any point where all of the weight of that body is concentrated — at any particular time. The center of gravity is different when we stand, sit, or bend. Anyone who skis or skates or dances knows how you must continually change your position to maintain balance: With movement, your center of gravity is constantly varying. The skyhook balances on your fingertip because the belt has pulled the concentrated weight, or center of gravity, to a point below your finger. As long as that point stays below your finger, you can balance the skyhook.

STATIC CEREAL BOX

All material things are made up of tiny particles called atoms. Every atom contains three types of particles: electrons, which are negative particles of electricity; protons, which are positive particles; and neutrons, which have no electrical charge. Electrons move about in many atoms; protons and neutrons are stationary. Generally, an object or matter has an equal number of electrons and protons, so the positive and negative charges cancel out each other. But when an object is rubbed, the electrons begin to move about and the friction created will rub electrons off one object and onto another. One object then gains more electrons, making it negatively charged.

The balloon you rubbed on your sleeve gained electrons from your sleeve's fabric and became negatively charged. As the balloon comes in contact with the neutral wall, it pushes that section of the wall's electrons away (like magnets, negative charges repel negative charges) and leaves more protons on that part of the wall, which becomes positively charged. Since opposites attract, the balloon sticks to the wall — for a while. After a bit, the negative electrons pass onto the wall from the balloon, and it falls.

Though the cereal in the box was neutral, rubbing caused the box top to become charged. That created an attraction (like the balloon and the wall) and made the cereal jump up to the cover. Touching the box top grounded the pieces of cereal and caused them to jump away, or be repelled.

STORMY SEAS SODA BOTTLE

Water has been called the universal solvent because so many other liquids and solids can be dissolved in it. Oil, however, cannot mix with water. When we shake the Stormy Seas Soda Bottle, little droplets of oil are suspended and spread through the blue water. More shaking will produce smaller droplets of oil. However, if left to sit for a while, the oil droplets cling together to re-form into one solid layer.

3/16 in = .48 cm	1 in = 2.54 cm	4 in = 10.2 cm	1/3 C = .08 l	1 l = 1.1 qt
1/4 in = .64 cm	1 1/2 in = 3.8 cm	6 in = 15.2 cm	1/2 C = .12 l	2 l = 2.1 qt
3/4 in = 1.9 cm	2 in = 5.1 cm	12 in = 30.5 cm	1 pt = .47 l	

BOATS AFLOAT

BOATS AFLOAT

1 lb = .45 kg	20 in = 50.8 cm
1 in = 2.54 cm	1 qt = .95 l
3 in = 7.6 cm	1 1/4 C = .3 l
10 in = 25.4 cm	2 C = .48 l

Planning an ocean voyage? Maybe you'd better take an hour to try this experiment before you set sail!

YOU WILL NEED

Plasticine or florist's clay
1 or 2 Large pots, pans, or basins
1 Pound of 1" finishing nails, or 2 or 3 dozen marbles all the same size, or box of paper clips
Cookie cutter or jar lid
1¼ Cups salt
2 Cups cooking oil
2 Bottle caps, 20" string, tape, long (1" or more) pin, plastic soda straw, 2 tall drinking glasses

Drop a steel nail into the water and it sinks right to the bottom. So how is it possible that a huge steel ship floats? You may think it has something to do with air trapped in compartments in the bottom of the ship. A little research will tell you if this is true or not.

1 Roll a piece of Plasticine or clay into a ball about the size of a golf ball. What happens when you drop the ball into a pot of water? Now take the ball and form it into a flat boat shape. Then take some small objects like nails, marbles, or paper clips and drop them in the boat. How many weights will your boat hold before it sinks? Now mold the same piece of Plasticine or clay into different boat shapes. What is the most any of these boats can hold and still float? What shape of boat seems to be able to carry the most?

2 Now organize a contest to see whose boat can carry the biggest load. Use a cookie cutter or jar lid to cut pieces of Plasticine or clay that are all the same size. Give each person a piece and have them build their own boats. Make up some contest rules. You'll have to decide when a loaded boat is still considered "floating": when it is halfway above the water, a quarter of the way, or just slightly under the water? Must the boat stay afloat for a minute or two after the last weight is added?

3 Try this contest: Who can build the smallest boat able to keep one marble afloat? You may need to make a balance to help you decide the winner of this contest. (See, Making a Balance, on this page.)

4 See how saltwater can affect your ships' ability to float. Mix 1¼ cups of salt with 1 quart of water (double these amounts if you need to). Let the saltwater stand for a while before you work with it. Meanwhile, float one boat in freshwater and write down how many weights it can carry. Then put the same boat in the saltwater. Does the number of weights change? (Saltwater can be rough on your hands, so use a plastic spoon to fish your boats and weights out.)

5 Now you've learned that the type of water itself works in helping boats float. But what would happen if you used 2 cups of cooking oil instead of water? How many weights can your boat carry then?

MAKING A BALANCE

1. Cut the 20" string in two. Cross the two 10" strings on top of a bottle cap and tape them in place. Turn the bottle cap over and pick up the four ends of the strings. Knot them together about 3" away from the cap. This is one *balance pan.*

2. Make another balance pan. Then hang one on each end of a plastic soda straw. Tape them in place. Push a long pin through the center, halfway down the straw. Stand two drinking glasses or jars close enough together so that the pin can rest on both rims and the balance can move freely. (Wiggle the pin back and forth a few times if the hole seems too tight.)

3. If your balance isn't exactly level when it is empty, stick bits of Plasticine or clay on the higher pan until it is level with the other. When you are trying to find out whose boat is smallest for Experiment Step

3, put a boat in each of the pans. When you see which is the lighter boat, leave it in one pan and set another boat in the second pan. Continue to weigh the boats against each other until you find the lightest one—the winner!

AFTERWORDS

Archimedes is probably the most famous bather of all time. He lived in Sicily more than 2,000 years ago and was a friend of the king. The king suspected that his new crown was not pure gold and asked Archimedes to investigate.

Archimedes could find out easily how much the crown weighed, but he didn't know how to calculate its *volume* (the amount of space it took up). As the story goes, Archimedes was lowering himself into his filled bathtub when he noticed the water spilling over the sides. Supposedly he was so excited by his discovery that he ran into the street yelling, *"Eureka!"* ("I have found it!"—the answer to his problem). He then dropped the crown into a full basin of water, catching the overflow. Next he weighed it against an equal volume of pure gold.

2 TALL DRINKING GLASSES — PIN

SALT

NAILS

SALT WATER

SALAD OIL

PAPER CLIP

TAPE PAPER TO TOOTH PICK TO MAKE A SAIL

MARBLE

His demonstration for the king showed that the pure gold was heavier than the "gold" crown, thus proving that it had been mixed with a lighter, cheaper metal. Some detective work!

When a ship is lowered into water, it *displaces* the water, pushing it out of the way. It does this until the weight of the displacement equals the weight of the ship — and the ship floats. Remember how your ball of Plasticine or clay sank? But after you flattened it out and turned up the edges, it floated. The shape of the thinner hull was able to displace enough water to equal the weight of the Plasticine plus its load.

Up until about 100 years ago, a ship's owner could have loaded his vessel with as much as he pleased. Many overloaded ships and their crews were lost when the boats sank in storms at sea. Then, in 1876, Samuel Plimsoll persuaded the British government to pass a law to control the loading of ships. The law required that every ship be marked with a horizontal line on its side to show the safe loading limit.

C = Coastal Service
TF = Tropical Freshwater
T = Tropical
F = Freshwater
S = Summer
W = Winter
WNA = Winter North Atlantic
AB = American Bureau of Shipping (the authority that decides where the marks should be)

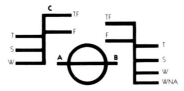

Notice that the Plimsoll marks also show the safe-loading limits for ships in different kinds of water and in different seasons. That's because, if you have two identical buckets and fill one with saltwater and the other with freshwater, the saltwater will weigh more. Saltwater is more *dense,* therefore heavier, than freshwater. Also, a bucket of warm saltwater from the Gulf of Mexico will weigh less than the same bucket filled with cold North Atlantic saltwater because cold water is more dense than warm water. Water temperatures also change according to the season.

Remember that a loaded ship floats because it displaces its own weight? Well, in dense waters (cold or saltwater), the ship won't sink as low into the water. In warm or non-salty waters, the ship has to displace *more* water in order to float. So, if an ocean vessel loses its way and happens to chug up the freshwater Mississippi River, it will sink lower into the water.

HIGH FLIERS

HIGH FLIERS

1/8 in = .32 cm	12 in = 30.5 cm
1/4 in = .64 cm	24 in = 60.9 cm
1/2 in = 1.27 cm	27 in = 68.6 cm
4 in = 10.2 cm	
8.5 in x 11 in = 22 cm x 27.9 cm	

Hats off to windy days! A blast of wind can give your spirits a lift. It only takes 20 minutes to experiment with a few low fliers, but you'll need 2 hours to build a high-flying kite of your own.

YOU WILL NEED

Hair blow-dryer
Several 8½" × 11" pieces of paper
Scissors, ruler, pencil
Kite line (20-pound test)
1 Sheet of 27" × 27" tissue paper, airplane paper, or crepe paper
3 Hardwood or softwood strips, each ¼" square × 24" long
Elmer's white glue
Rubber cement
Sharp utility knife or small saw
Paints for decoration (optional)
1 Small plastic ring (available in the drapery section of a department store)
Needle with large eye

Have you ever seen a round kite? Do you think a round kite would fly? There's only one way to find out — experiment! The best kite shapes will create a reaction in the air around them. This reaction is called *lift*. You get lift when the pressure on top of a kite — or bird or plane — is less than the pressure underneath it. In High Fliers, you can "test fly" many flat shapes in your living room to find out which ones will soar. Then make a kite and fly it, to feel the power of the wind in your hands. That should give *you* the biggest lift of all!

TEST FLIGHTS

1 Plug in the blow-dryer near a table. The table is going to be your testing runway. Put a sheet of paper down flat on the runway, three inches from the edge of the table. Hold the blow-dryer several inches above the table and turn it on to the low setting. You might have to move the hair-dryer around a little bit to get the angle right, but very soon the paper should lift off and "fly" across the table.

2 Cut out a circle, a diamond, an oval, a hexagon, and several other shapes from the remaining pieces of paper. Try to make all the shapes about the same size. Test fly each shape on your runway, and try to decide which shape flies best. **Note:** Don't expect the shapes to fly very high. Half an inch off the table would be an excellent flight height!

3 Repeat the experiment, but this time crumple up one or more of the paper shapes first. Do the crumpled pieces lift off the table?

A HIGH-FLYING KITE

4 To get your project "off the ground," you have to make a kite frame. Use a sharp utility knife to cut a shallow (⅛") square notch in the center of two of the hardwood or softwood strips. These strips are called *spars*. (They go from side to side across the kite to give it support.) Cut square notches four inches in from each end of the third wooden strip.

This strip is called the *spine*. (It goes from top to bottom, and is the kite's "backbone.")

WARNING! MAKE V-NOTCH IN RELATION TO SQ. NOTCH

5 Now you will need to make V-shaped notches in the ends of the spars and the spine. Later you will be running a piece of kite string around the kite frame through these V-notches, so be sure that the V-notches are going in the right direction. The diagram shows you how the V-notches should look in relation to the square notches you already made.

6 Latch the spars to the spine to form the kite shape shown. To latch them together, first put some

TIE STRING IN CRISS-CROSS FASHION

Elmer's glue in the square notches and fit them together. Then use a piece of kite line to tie the spars to the spine at the square notches. Tie the string in a crisscross fashion, going around one way and then the other. When you have finished latching, pour a small amount of glue over the strings, and let it dry.

7 Tie a piece of 20-pound-test kite line to one end of the center spine, hooking the line into the V-

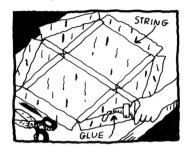

STRING

GLUE

notch. Run the kite line all the way around the frame through the V-notches, pulling it tight but not tight enough to bend or snap the spars. Tie the kite-

line ends together when you get back to the beginning, at the center spine. Adjust the frame until it is "squared up"

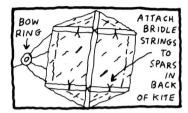

BOW RING

ATTACH BRIDLE STRINGS TO SPARS IN BACK OF KITE

and symmetrical, so that the spars and spine meet in a right (90°) angle.

8 Using the frame as a pattern, cut a kite cover from the 27" × 27" piece of paper. Be sure to *allow one inch extra* all around for a "hem." Cut slits at each corner of the cover, where the spars and spine are. Fold each edge over the outline string and glue it in place using rubber cement. Follow the tradi-

tion of kite-makers everywhere by decorating your kite boldly, using *lots* of color.

9 Make a bridle by attaching four pieces of kite line, 12″ each, to the spars as shown in the diagram. You can use a needle with a large eye to do this. The bridle goes on the front of the kite, so you'll have to poke small holes in the cover and stick the line through it to tie the bridle on. You may reinforce the cover with Scotch tape if you want to, but use only a small amount of tape right near the bridle holes. Tie all four bridle lines to a tow ring—a small, lightweight plastic ring like the ones used on drapery and curtain rods. Then tie the rest of the kite line to the tow line…and go fly your kite!

TIPS FOR KITE MAKERS

■ Make your kite as light as possible.
■ Before constructing your kite, be sure the spars are balanced. Measure to find their exact centers, and then balance each spar on one fingertip. Shave off small pieces if necessary.
■ If your kite won't fly, adjust the bridle. Make it shorter or

longer. Or attach it somewhere else along the spars. (Cover over the old holes with small pieces of tape.) Keep trying!

AFTERWORDS

For more than 2,000 years, the people of China, Japan, Korea, and many parts of Asia have been flying elaborate kites — most often for pleasure, but sometimes with other purposes as well. Fishermen from China and Japan have been seen standing on shore with a kite flown out to sea. Dangling from the kite line is another string, which falls into the water several hundred feet from shore. When the fishermen feel the kite pulling away, they reel it in and collect a fish at the end of the second line! For sport, Koreans apply a mixture of glue and crushed glass or sand to the kite line near the kite, and engage in kite fighting. The object is to direct one's kite line toward an opponent's kite, cross the kite lines, and cut his line with a quick jerking motion. So proud are the Chinese of their kite-flying traditions that they set aside a holiday in September, called Kite Day. Similarly, the Japanese fly kites on Boy's Day in May, and the Koreans

celebrate the first day of the new year with kites flown from morning until night.

Finally, in the 18th century, kites were put to scientific use. Two young Scottish students, Alexander Wilson and Thomas Melville, attached a thermometer to a kite and flew it to test their hypothesis that air is colder at higher altitudes. Three years later, in 1752, Ben Franklin discovered the presence of electricity in the air by flying a kite during a thunderstorm. He had tied the kite line to a key, and tied the key to a silk ribbon, which he held. He was gambling that if the ribbon remained dry, he would not receive an electrical shock. In fact, the electricity traveled down the kite line to the key, and jumped across the space between the key and his hand, giving him a small shock.

In the late 1800s, another Scotsman, Captain B.F.S. Baden-Powell, developed a way to lift a man into the air in a basket attached to six kites flown in tandem. The kites were hexagonal ones, called Levitors. (The kite you made in High Fliers is a Levitor kite!) Baden-Powell's man-lifting kite was soon adopted by the army and used during

the Boer War for aerial observations.

Next, William A. Eddy designed the first kite to use a bowed, or bent, spar. The Eddy kite had better lifting qualities than earlier kites, and it was more stable too. When Eddy presented his kite design to the U.S. Weather Bureau in 1894, they immediately saw the potential for lifting meteorological instruments into the sky, and weather stations continued to use kites until more modern methods replaced them.

Perhaps the most dramatic development in the history of kites came from Lawrence Hargrave, an Australian who invented the box kite, which bears his name. The box kite was shaped just like a rectangular box, open at both ends and in the middle of the remaining four sides. Even in rough winds and bad weather conditions, it proved to be an extremely stable, high-flying kite. Then, Orville and Wilbur Wright turned the box kite on its side, twisted the flat surfaces somewhat, and used it as the basis for the wing span on their first manned flying machine!

JUST PLANE WINGS

JUST PLANE WINGS

6. PAPER CLIP

Don't be a sore loser—be a *soaring* winner, with these paper airplanes that help you reach new heights. It will take you only a few minutes to make your airplanes, but you may want to test-fly them all day!

YOU WILL NEED

Several sheets of 8½" by 11" paper
Paper clips
Ruler
Scissors
Plastic straws

What one thing do jet fighters, bumblebees, bluejays, and paper airplanes all have in common? The answer is wings, of course. Wings are the one thing you've got to have if you're going to fly. But don't be surprised if some wings look a little bit different from others!

STUNT FLYER

This is the best paper airplane ever! It will loop-the-loop, do a barrel roll, or glide for long distances on a gentle breeze. And best of all, it has a snub nose, so you can zoom it at your friends without hurting anyone.

1 Start with an 8½" by 11" piece of paper. Fold it in half lengthwise, then open the paper up again. Bring the two top corners to meet on the middle fold, as in diagram 1. Then fold the top triangle down across line A-B, as in diagram 2.

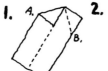

2 Fold up the point of the triangle, point C, so that it is about an inch long, as in diagram 3.

3 Now fold points A and B in toward the center line, so that they meet on top of the small triangle. They should touch the triangle a little less than halfway up from its fold. See diagram 4.

3.

4.

4 Bring the folded edges of the plane (line X and line Y on the diagram) to meet in the middle. Diagram 5 shows the airplane after one side has been folded in. The dotted line shows where the other side will be folded.

5.

5 Now the paper airplane is ready to fly! Simply fold it in half lengthwise, along the center line, and hold the airplane from underneath. The snub-nosed end is the front, of course. Fly the airplane as it is a few times, and then add a paper clip just under the nose. Does your plane fly better with or without the paper clip? Where does the clip work best? When you try the stunts below, be sure to try them with and without the paper clip.

Stunts

■ To make your stunt plane do a barrel roll, bend or curl one tail piece *up* about an inch, and bend or curl the other tail piece *down* about an inch.

■ To loop-the-loop (your plane will curve down and come back to you), bend both tail pieces down. It may take some practice to throw the Stunt Flyer properly. If you want it to come right back to your hand, aim upward when you throw it.

■ The Stunt Flyer can loop-the-loop the opposite way—by curving up and around—and then it will keep on going! To do this stunt, bend both tail pieces up, and snap your wrist when you fly the plane. It will take some practice, but it's worth it!

HELICOPTER

This paper flyer moves just like the blades of a helicopter. Try making very small paper helicopters and very large ones. Stand on a chair and drop two different ones at the same time. Do they both descend at the same speed?

1 To make a paper helicopter, cut a strip of paper 11" long and 2" wide. Following the diagram, cut along the solid lines. There are only three cuts to be made. Cut #1 is 5" long, and the other two cuts are each about ⅔" long.

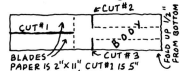

2 Now make the two long folds, along the dotted lines. These folds cause the body of the helicopter to be folded in thirds, with the two sides overlapping the center. Fold the bottom of the helicopter up a half inch and then

another half inch, to make the bottom heavier. You can also put a paper clip on the bottom to weight it.

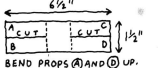

3 Last, fold the blades of the helicopter in opposite directions. One should point toward you and the other should point away.

4 Drop your helicopter from a high place, or stand on a chair and let it go. What makes it twirl? How is your helicopter different from a real helicopter? *Hint:* Can your helicopter ever go *up*?

WHIRLY TWIRLER

You can make a Whirly Twirler with only a drinking straw

and a small piece of paper.

1 Cut or tear a piece of paper to make a rectangle about 1½" wide and 6½" long. Fold the

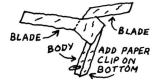

paper in half lengthwise. Cut or tear along the fold from each end toward the middle, leaving the center of the paper untorn. Now you have

four propellers.

2 Bend one propeller up and the other down on one side of the paper. Bend the opposite propellers up and down on the other side of the paper, as shown in the diagram.

3 Poke the straw through the center of the paper and your Whirly Twirler is done! Let it fall from a high place and see whether it spins faster or slower than the paper helicopter.

1/2 in = 1.27 cm	2 in = 5.1 cm
2/3 in = 1.69 cm	5 in = 12.7 cm
1 in = 2.54 cm	6 1/2 in = 16.5 cm
1 1/4 in = 3.2 cm	7 in = 17.8 cm
1 1/2 in = 3.8 cm	9 in = 22.9 cm
8.5 in x 11 in =	11 in = 27.9 cm
22 cm x 28 cm	

1 Cut one paper strip 7" long and the other strip 9" long. Make the strips into loops by overlapping the ends about an inch or so and taping them closed.

TAPE LOOPS TO STRAW

2 Next tape the loops to the straw, as shown. Where are the wings? To fly this plane, hold it with the smaller loop facing forward, and the straw on the bottom. It will glide and sometimes even spiral as it soars across your living room.

ROCKET BOMBER

Can a rolled-up piece of notebook paper fly? Try it and find out.

1 Take an 8½" by 11" sheet of paper and roll it into a tube with a 1" diameter. Use tape to keep it closed. Try to fly it across the room.

2 Now roll up another piece of paper the same way and tape it closed. Cut a 2" slash in one end. Cut sideways from the

slash in two directions, so that a tail is formed, as in the diagram.

CUT HERE TO FORM TAIL

3 Fly the Rocket Bomber with the tail toward the back. Does the Rocket Bomber have wings? Do real rockets have wings? Do they have tails?

AFTERWORDS

For thousands of years, people have wanted to be able to fly like the birds. But have they succeeded? Technically, no! Even today, no one has mastered the art of flying the way birds do: by flapping their wings.

Flapping wings are unique to birds, although many people have tried—and failed—to imitate them. Still scientists dreamed of flight for many years. Leonardo da Vinci made a drawing of a design for a helicopter—almost 500 years before it was invented! And Sir Isaac Newton understood the principles of flight, but he ended up

predicting that people would never fly!

Modern scientists have studied the flapping motion of birds' wings, and found out just how tricky flapping flight is. For one thing, a bird's wing does not merely go up and down in two evenly timed movements. The downward motion is smooth and slow, while the upward motion is faster and includes a flicking motion. If you watch a bird flying, you'll notice that it's easier to see the wings' downbeat, because it lasts longer.

Although no one has mastered flapping flight, airplanes do glide and soar using some of the same design elements found on birds. An airplane's wings are curved at the front and tapered at the back, like a bird's. And flaps on an airplane wing can be moved up or down to increase the curvature of the wing during takeoff and landing. Those adjustments are similar to the changes you made when you changed the position of the tail pieces on your paper airplane. Of course you can only make a *few* adjustments

in the wings or tail pieces of your paper flyers, compared with the *hundreds* of tiny adjustments that birds make.

Another similarity between birds, planes, and paper airplanes is the need for a tail. The tail is used for steering and for balance. Without a tail, birds and planes would tend to go topsy-turvy and take an unscheduled nose dive. That's probably what happened to your Rocket Bomber when it was just a paper tube without a tail.

Whether you're flying a paper Stunt Flyer or a DC-10 commercial jet, the principles of flight remain the same. The airplane must go fast enough to create something called *lift*. Lift is the result of air flowing over the wings of a plane at a great speed. The air pressure above the wing is less than the air pressure below the wing, so the plane goes up. Why can't your paper airplane just glide on forever? Because it doesn't have a motor … and as it starts to slow down, the air pressure above the wing increases. No more lift— and no more flight!

SKYDIVER

SKYDIVER

4 T = 60 ml	3 in = 7.6 cm
6 T = 90 ml	12 in = 30.5 cm
1/4 in = .64 cm	23 ft = 7 m
1/2 in = 1.27 cm	6,000 ft = 1,829 m

What goes up must come down—but wearing a parachute makes landing easier! This activity will take 30 minutes, plus a few hours drying time for your papier-mâché paratrooper.

YOU WILL NEED

Small piece of cardboard
Scissors
Pipe cleaners
Flour
Water
Bowl and spoon
Newspapers
Tempera or hobby paints
Paintbrush
Plastic from garbage bags,
  dry-cleaning bags,
  or food-storage bags
Felt-tip marker
Needle
Heavy-duty thread

Did you know that even the most experienced paratroopers sometimes get hurt when parachuting out of an airplane? As the saying goes: "It's not the fall that hurts—it's the landing." Maybe you've wondered why these paratroopers hit the ground so hard.

It seems like there should be some way to keep them from falling so fast. Well, you'll find out why parachutes are designed the way they are when you make your own test pilot who's heading for a fall!

1 Cut out a body for your parachute man from a small piece of cardboard, using the pattern shown here. Your man should be about the same size as the pattern.

USE THIS FOR PATTERN AND PAINT YOUR OWN PARACHUTIST

2 Make a "loop" by twisting a pipe cleaner into the shape of a script *e*, as shown. (Later you'll tie your parachute to this loop.)

Place the loop against the cardboard man's neck so that the two tails of pipe cleaner stick out to form arms. Then wrap the arms around the neck once to attach the pipe cleaner to the man. This is the

MAKE SURE LOOP IS AWAY FROM BODY AND FREE TO TIE STRING TO IT.

frame for the parachute man.

3 Mix up some papier-mâché paste by combining 4 tablespoons flour with 6 tablespoons water in a small bowl. Cut or tear strips of newspaper about ½" wide. Dip a strip of newspaper into the paste and then use your fingers to wipe off the excess. Cover the arms, head, and body of the parachute man with strips of papier-mâché wrapping them around and around to

build up a little bulk. **But be sure to leave the loop free and uncovered!** Let the papier-mâché man dry for a few hours or overnight. Then you can paint a face and overalls on your parachutist.

FLO

BE SURE LOOP IS FREE

4 While the paint is drying, cut a circle out of lightweight plastic such as a garbage bag, food-storage bag, or the plastic that covers your clothes when they come back from the dry cleaner. This will be your parachute. How big a parachute will you need? Do you think a parachute could ever be *too* big? You'll find out by experimenting with circles of various sizes. If your man is less than 3" tall, you can start with a parachute 12" in diameter.

5 Now it's time to attach the lines to the parachute, and then to the man. First, look at your parachute circle and pretend it is a clock. With a felt-tip marker, put a dot each, about ¼" from the parachute edge, at 12 o'clock, 2 o'clock, 4 o'clock, 6 o'clock, 8 o'clock, and 10 o'clock. Thread a needle with a single strand of heavy-duty thread and attach six lines to the parachute, one at each dot, as shown in the diagram. How long should the lines be?

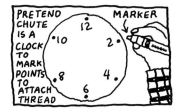

PRETEND CHUTE IS A CLOCK TO MARK POINTS TO ATTACH THREAD

MARKER

12
•10   •2
•8   •4
6

That depends on the size of your parachute. A good rule of thumb is to make the lines approximately as long as the parachute is wide. Once you have threaded the lines through the plastic, though, they will be double strands — half the width of the para-

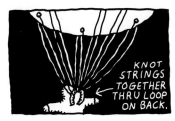

KNOT STRINGS TOGETHER THRU LOOP ON BACK.

chute. When all six lines are attached to the chute, pull them together and make sure that they are all *exactly* the same length. Knot them through the loop on the back of the parachute man's neck, as if they were all one thick cord.

6 Time to bail out! Experiment with your parachute man by tossing him into the air, or dropping him from the top of a ladder. But if you're going to climb a ladder, be sure to have an

adult nearby. You also can throw your parachute man out a window, but **never lean out the window!** Have a friend waiting below to watch where it lands.

When you drop him from a high place, does your parachute man fall gently to the ground or does he plummet to the earth? Does he swing from side to side as he descends? If so, cut a small hole — a little smaller than a dime — in the very center of the chute. This air vent helps stabilize the parachute's descent. Experiment with different-size chutes on the same man. Can you figure out why paratroopers don't want huge parachutes, even though bigger chutes would allow them to land more gently?

VARIATIONS

■ Attach the parachute man to a helium balloon and let it go. When the helium balloon gets high enough, it will explode, and the man will parachute to earth. This is how one of the first parachutists got the chance to test his new invention! If you write your name and address on the parachute in permanent marker before launching the balloon, you might get a letter or call from the person who finds it.

■ Before tying the lines (threads) to the man, arrange them so that one is shorter than the others. How does this affect the parachute man's fall?

AFTERWORDS

Imagine: Long before people had thought of a way to get themselves up off the ground, Leonardo da Vinci had devised a way to land safely: with a parachute. His drawing of a man descending in a square-framed parachute dates from around 1485 — a full 300 years before human beings first took to the skies in hot-air balloons! But in 1783, a Frenchman named Sebastien Lenormand actually built a parachute and tried it out himself by jumping from a tower in Paris. He survived, and is usually credited with having invented the parachute.

Ten years later, another Frenchman, André-Jacques Garnerin, constructed a parachute of white linen, 23 feet in diameter, and attached it to a hot-air balloon. Then he went up to 6,000 feet and cut the hot-air balloon free! As crowds of awestruck people watched silently from the ground, Garnerin came down. His descent was successful, but because his parachute had been designed without an air vent, he was swung violently from side to side. He fainted from the nauseating experience!

Parachutes wouldn't be necessary at all if it weren't for one thing: gravity. Gravity is the force that attracts two bodies to each other — any two bodies, although most of the time we are only aware of the Earth's gravity. Did you know that the force of gravity is present between everything — even between you and your lamp? It's just that it is very, very weak gravity — so weak that no matter how close you get to your lamp, it won't fall on you from the force of your own gravitational pull! Here's why: The mathematical equation that explains the force of gravity says basically that the force of gravity increases when the distance between the two bodies decreases. But it also says that the *mass* of the two bodies — how dense they are and how much they weigh — has a lot to do with how strong the gravitational force is. You and your lamp — or any other objects you get close to — don't weigh enough *together* to create a noticeable gravitational force.

Of course, there's gravity on the moon, too, but its force is not as powerful as the Earth's. That's why you weigh less on the moon than you do on Earth. Some people think that gravity is weaker on the moon because it's "way out in space." But that's not true. Gravity is weaker on the moon because the moon is smaller than Earth, and so it's gravitational pull on a human being is less. The moon would be a great place to practice parachuting. Even if your parachute didn't open, it wouldn't hurt half so much when you came down!

Stars, too, are subject to the laws of gravity, and they exert an enormous force on the smaller bodies around them. Take our sun, for instance, which is really a very near star. The sun has so much mass, it is able to attract the Earth and the other planets, and hold them in its power! If the sun were smaller and much less dense, the Earth would never have been pulled into orbit around the sun. It might have flown out into space and become a meteoroid instead. If the sun were larger and more dense, the Earth would be pulled right *to* the sun by the force of the sun's gravity, and burn up. Isn't it amazing that the sun's mass is just right to maintain its safe gravitational relationship with Earth?

FOR THE BIRDS

FOR THE BIRDS

1/2 in = 1.27 cm	5 in = 12.7 cm
5 ft = 1.5 m	2 l = 2.1 qt
1/4 C = .06 l	1 C = .24 l
2 in = 5.1 cm	1 qt = .95 l

You don't need to take out an ad in the *Bird Gazette* to let the birds in your neighborhood know that you care! Just put out a bird feeder. It will take about 30 minutes to make a simple feeder. Then you can watch the action for hours.

YOU WILL NEED

Empty milk carton, soda bottle, or bleach bottle
Duct tape or other heavy, waterproof tape
Scissors or knife
Pipe cleaners
Popsicle sticks
Colored paper for decorating feeder
Glue
Rope or clothesline
Birdseed

In winter, the insects, seeds, and berries that songbirds eat are scarce, and snow often covers the ground. Many birds will starve or freeze if they don't find enough food to eat. You can make a bird feeder and put it in your yard, in a park, or out along the roadside, to help feed the winter birds. Do it now, because that way the birds will learn to come to your feeder before the cold weather arrives. And keep your feeder filled into the spring, because the birds have learned to count on you for food!

If you live in a warmer part of the country, you're lucky. Many songbirds are there all year round. Having a bird feeder is a great way to meet them!

1 Wash out an empty 1-quart milk carton, a 2-liter soda bottle, and/or an empty bleach bottle with a handle. *Be sure the container is well rinsed before you begin.*

2 Seal the original opening with duct tape. If you are using a milk carton, close it and tape the top tightly shut. If you are using a plastic bottle, screw the cap on tightly and seal with duct tape. Remove any labels from the bottle.

3 With your scissors, cut a small door or opening in the container about 5 inches from the bottom. There are lots of ways to construct a feeder. If you are using a soda bottle, you can lay it on its side and call that the bottom. In that case, you might want to make two doors. They can open sideways, like a door, or upwards, like a tent flap. Make the doors small if you want to discourage larger birds: Large birds sometimes scare the smaller birds away. If you make a huge hole in your feeder, you'll probably end up feeding squirrels instead!

4 Tie the door open with a pipe cleaner. Put a small hole in the door and a small hole in the feeder. Put a pipe cleaner through the hole in the door and knot it or twist it. Put the other end through the hole in the bottle and knot it.

5 Make a perch for the birds to stand on when they come to your bird feeder. You will need two Popsicle sticks for each perch. Use scissors or a knife to make a small slit about ½" below the opening in the feeder. Make another slit about ½" below the first slit. Push one Popsicle stick through each slit until only about 2" of each stick remains outside the feeder. Tape the two sticks together with duct tape to form a wedge-shaped perch. (If using a milk carton, also decorate the outside of your feeder: Glue on some colored paper.)

6 You will need to make handles or straps to hang up your bird feeder. Where you put the handles will depend on what style of feeder you designed. For a bleach-bottle bird feeder, you can simply put a rope through the handle and suspend it from a tree branch. For a soda bottle turned on its side or for a milk carton, you will need two pipe-cleaner handles—one at each end of the top of your feeder. Poke two holes in the top left side of your feeder and push one pipe cleaner through both of them. Twist the ends together or knot them. Do the same at the right end of the top.

7 Fill your bird feeder with seeds. Make sure the birdseeds come all the way up to the opening, so that small birds can reach them—without having to climb *into* the bottle!

8 Make two or more feeders and find out which kind the birds like best. Do they want to be able to see the seeds inside? Or are they more attracted to a colorfully decorated bird feeder? Even if you made two bird feeders, use the same kind of birdseed in each one. That way you will know that it is the difference in shape or color of the bottle—and not the food inside—that explains why birds do or don't come to each feeder. Later, you can experiment with different kinds of food.

WHERE TO HANG YOUR BIRD FEEDER

Bird feeders should be hung at least 5 feet from the ground, so that dogs and cats cannot reach the birds while they are feeding. You'll also want to hang the feeder away from bushes or benches, so that squirrels cannot jump to the bird feeder and eat all the food. Suspend the feeder from a wire attached to a tree limb…or hang it from a clothesline.

WHAT TO FEED THE BIRDS

What do birds like to eat? Different birds like different kinds of seed. Many birds will also eat bread crumbs, fruits, nuts, and suet (beef fat). This list will help you decide what kind of food to use.

Bread Crumbs: Scatter fresh white bread crumbs (or small pieces of white bread) on the ground to attract birds.

Black-striped Sunflower Seeds: These seeds will attract bluejays, chickadees, grosbeaks, tufted titmice, finches, and cardinals.

Mixed Seeds: This is the most easily available kind of birdseed.

Fruits: Put out some raisins, apple slices, pieces of banana, and orange slices, especially in summer.

Suet: This beef fat is available in the grocery store. It will attract woodpeckers, which eat insects in summer.

Roasted Peanuts (in the shell): These are good for bluejays.

USE **2** POPSICLE STICKS TO MAKE PERCH

DECORATE MILK CARTON

HANG FEEDERS AT LEAST **5** FEET FROM GROUND

USE PIPE CLEANERS TO HANG FEEDERS WITHOUT HANDLES

BIRD SEED

Peanut Butter: Plain peanut butter is too thick for birds to swallow. Use 1 cup of cornmeal to every ¼ cup of peanut butter. Add enough vegetable shortening to make it less sticky. You can smear the mixture directly on a tree trunk, or on a pinecone and hang it from a tree.

Water: Birds need water, so put out a saucer for them, or fill one of your extra feeders with water and cut a larger opening. Change the water frequently.

Grit: Mix a little sand or grit in with your birdseed. Birds must have grit to digest their food. They also like crushed eggshells for the calcium they contain.

CARE FOR YOUR FEEDER

Don't let the birdseed in your feeder get wet, soggy, or moldy. Birds can get a deadly disease from eating wet birdseed. Clean out the feeder and scrub it well about once a week—or make a new feeder with another soda bottle. It's easy!

AFTERWORDS

Have you ever heard someone say, "You're eating like a bird?" They probably meant that you weren't eating much. But birds actually eat quite a lot. In fact, most songbirds will eat many times a day— especially in winter, when they need the extra fuel to keep warm. And birds getting ready to migrate can double their own body weight in only a few days! They store up fat to use as fuel for their journey south.

But if adult birds eat a lot, baby birds eat *more*, especially just before they leave the nest. They must be fed *every 15 to 30 minutes* during the first few weeks of life! Their parents spend the whole day flying back and forth to the nest, bringing food. The baby that stretches its neck up the farthest and opens its mouth the widest is always fed first. That's just nature's way of making sure the hungriest bird gets what it needs.

Birds have excellent eyesight, which is how they find food. Did birds come to feed more quickly at your clear plastic soda-bottle feeder than at your less-transparent feeders? That's because they spotted the food from the air.

Of course, not all birds eat seeds, but birds of prey such as vultures and eagles also rely on their eyesight to lead them to food. Some owls' and eagles' eyes are actually larger than human eyes, and hawks are thought to see *10 times* better than human beings. Birds have superior vision for a number of reasons. They have a double set of muscles so they can focus more easily on objects at different distances. They also have more cones and rods—the cells in the eye that are sensitive to color and light.

If you're not sure what a certain species of bird eats, you can often figure it out by looking at the bird's beak. Each beak shape is suited to a specific purpose: For instance, the hooked bill of a hawk is used for striking and killing prey animals. The woodpecker's pointed bill is used to dig insects out of trees. The cone-shaped beak found on many songbirds can crack open or crush seeds. And the long, tapered bill of the hummingbird is perfect for reaching deep into flowers and sucking out nectar.

Although seed-eating birds have no teeth, they do need to grind up their food, the way animals and people do when they chew. That's why these birds eat grit— sand or small pebbles. This gravel stays in the bird's stomach, or *gizzard*. When the digestive muscles go to work, grinding and mashing up the food, the gravel acts like a hard, grinding surface.

What do songbirds eat when people aren't feeding them? In summer, many birds eat seeds and berries that are plentiful then. The seeds from pine trees are one of their most important sources of food. They eat the berries from almost every kind of bush imaginable, and also like acorns and cherries. Most important of all, many birds eat insects. If it weren't for birds, the world would be overrun with insects! Some farmers and gardeners put up bird feeders to attract these insect-eaters. The birds then take up residence in the area and help to control the insects that would otherwise do a lot of damage to crops.

Thanks to birds, the balance of nature is maintained. And thanks to your bird feeder, many birds will live through a cold winter.

TURF
TICKERS

TURF TICKERS

12 in x 12 in = 30.5 cm x 30.5 cm
3/4 in = 1.9 cm
2 in = 5.1 cm   5 1/4 in = 13.3 cm
4 1/4 in = 10.8 cm   5 3/8 in = 13.7 cm

"A clock the time may
   wrongly tell;
I, never, if the sun
   shine well."

Rain or shine, it will take several hours to build a Turf Ticker sundial.

YOU WILL NEED

Corrugated cardboard from
   a carton
Scissors
Pencil
Protractor
Ruler or yardstick
Masking tape
Compass (optional)

There is an ancient, automatic timekeeper on your lawn every sunny day. Learn how to use it by building a Turf Ticker sundial. You can make this simple sundial with only a few parts. The sun shines onto the pointer or gnomon (NO-mon) of the sundial. The gnomon's shadow falls onto the dial plate. The dial plate has numbers on it (like a clock) that tell you the time.

Sundials have been used to tell time for centuries. People all over the world have designed different kinds of sundials. Even today, no formal garden is complete without one. Now you can create your own sundial, too.

1 Cut a piece of cardboard from a carton 12" × 12" or bigger — the bigger, the better. Fold the cardboard in half. You may want to score the fold slightly, so that it bends easily. Scoring means cutting the cardboard partway through with the point of a scissors, so it's easier to bend.

2 Using scissors, poke a hole in the top center of your dial plate about ¾" from the top edge. Make the hole just large enough to fit a pencil into it. This is your *gnomon hole*.

3 A protractor measures degrees of angles and circles like a ruler measures inches or straight lines. Find the small hole along the straight edge of your protractor. Lay the protractor on top of the dial plate with the straight edges parallel. Make sure the protractor's hole is right over the gnomon hole.

To label the dial plate, make a dot every 15 degrees

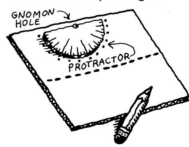

all the way around the protractor. Start at 0 degrees, then mark 30 degrees, 45 degrees, 60 degrees, and so on. Remove the protractor.

4 Using a ruler, draw lines from the gnomon hole to each of the dots. These are your hour lines. Label each hour line, starting at 6 A.M. on one side and going all the way around the semi-circle to 6 P.M. The line that goes straight up the middle, at 90 degrees, is 12 noon.

5 Make two triangles of cardboard to prop up the sundial at the correct angle for your latitude. For the sundial to work properly, the triangles must be made according to the instructions. See the map to decide which city is on approximately the same latitude as your hometown. For instance, if you live in Seattle or Minneapolis, use the dimensions shown for Bangor, Maine.

TRIANGLE INSTRUCTIONS

Make two right triangles. Right triangles are ones that have an L-shaped side, forming a 90-degree angle. The length of the sides will vary, depending on where you live. *See dimensions at right.* You will notice that when you change the length of the L sides, it changes the other angles. You can measure the angles with your protractor if you want to.

Attach the triangle wedges with tape to hold the dial plate open at the correct angle. The *bottom* of the L should be touching the bottom or base of the sundial.

The side of the right triangle that is opposite the L

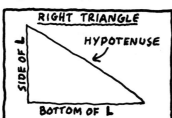

is called the *hypotenuse*. The hypotenuse should be touching the dial plate.

Triangle Dimensions

	Bottom of L	Side of L
Bangor, Maine:	5¼″	5¼″
Washington, D.C.:	4¼″	5⅜″
Miami, Florida:	2″	4¼″

6 Put the eraser end of the pencil in place in the gnomon hole. The pencil is now the gnomon. It should be set perpendicular to the dial plate. If you set the protractor flat on the dial plate, the pencil should line up with the 90-degree line.

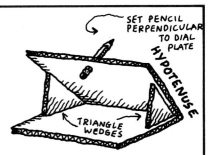

7 Find a sunny outdoor spot for your sundial. Find north with a compass and point your 12 noon line directly north. Or place the sundial so that the gnomon casts a shadow on the correct hour. Your noon line will be facing north.

ST/84

KEEPING TIME

In the spring and summer, *you* may be on daylight saving time, but the sun and your sundial *are not.* That means that your sundial will read 11 a.m. when your watch reads 12 noon. When you go back to standard time, your watch and sundial will agree again.

So make sure the hour you set your sundial with is standard time, *not* daylight saving time.

VARIATIONS

■ To weatherize your sundial, cover the parts with plastic wrap or clear contact paper.
■ Use your cardboard parts as a pattern to make a sundial out of wood. With a few layers of shellac, it will be waterproof.

AFTERWORDS

Every day, plant and animal activities repeat themselves as if they were on a schedule. Leaves fold up at night, birds sing at dawn, and we are hungry at noon. Less obvious, but equally regular, photosynthesis, cell division, and hormonal changes form daily patterns. These and the many other plant and animal activities that occur at approximately 24-hour intervals operate according to "circadian rhythms." *Circadian* comes from the Latin word *circa* meaning "about" and *dies* meaning "day."

Plants, insects, fish, birds, and humans all exhibit circadian rhythms. To find out more about the biological mechanism that causes circadian rhythms, scientists have lowered plants and animals into salt mines, shipped them to the South Pole and spun them on turntables, and orbited them in satellites. As a result of these efforts, most scientists agree that plants and animals have internal timing devices called "biological clocks." The chemical and physical nature of these clocks is not yet known.

Not every biological clock is set exactly for a 24-hour cycle. Some are as short as 21 hours and others as long as 27 hours. This difference can create problems. An insect with a 23-hour 25-minute rhythm will be five hours behind a plant with a strict 24-hour schedule in only 20 days. This may be just long enough for the insect to miss the few hours of the day when the plant's flower is open.

Fortunately, the environment helps synchronize these different rhythms. Many plants and animals respond to slight changes in the amount of daylight. For example, "long day" plants will only flower when there are many hours of daylight. Spinach will not grow in the tropics, because it needs at least 14 hours of light each day for two weeks, which never happens in the tropics. On the other hand, ragweed doesn't grow in northern Maine because it only flowers when there are less than 14½ hours of daylight. The days don't shorten that much in northern Maine until August, but then there isn't enough time for the seeds to develop before the first frost.

We, too, depend on light changes to set our biological clocks. The effects of "jet lag" are, in part, due to the different rates at which the different organs and functions of the human body adjust to new schedules. One gland may send a hormone to an organ that hasn't yet adjusted and isn't expecting any stimulus. Repeated jolts such as these may cause serious long-term effects. Similarly, a prescribed dose of medicine may cause different reactions at different times of day. A dose that will help in the morning may harm at night. The more we learn about circadian rhythms and biological clocks, the better we can understand reactions, adaptions, and evolution.

CASTS OF CHARACTERS

CASTS OF CHARACTERS

You can record what you can see and touch by taking pictures or making drawings. But there's another way that's longer lasting, more lifelike — and more fun! The casts can be made in about 20 minutes, plus an hour's drying time.

YOU WILL NEED

Door key
Plasticine or modeling clay
Paring knife
Some newspapers
Empty cardboard milk carton
6 Paper clips
2 Teaspoonfuls petroleum jelly (such as Vaseline)
Plaster of Paris, at least a pound (Buy the cheapest kind you can get. Drugstores sell small amounts; building supply stores sell large sacks.)
Empty half-gallon plastic ice-cream carton
Small, stiff brush (An old toothbrush will do.)
Stirring stick or wooden ruler, spoon
Paper towels and dish detergent

Paint, any kind: poster, watercolor, spray
Wire coat hangers

Suppose you are hiking in the Pacific Northwest and find some footprints — footprints of the legendary *Sasquatch,* "Bigfoot," the wildman of the Rockies. How can you bring back a footprint to prove to the rest of the world that you found him? You *could* take photographs, but here's a better way.

1 First, practice your technique! Start out with something smaller than a footprint — like a door key. Roll out a pad of Plasticine or clay about as big as your palm and about ½" thick. Put it on a pad of newspapers on the table. Use a paring knife to cut it into a round cookie shape.

2 Lay your key flat on the center of the Plasticine and press down hard. Make the top of the key level with the top of the Plasticine. Now, very carefully lift out the key.

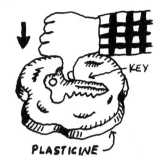

PLASTICINE

KEY

3 Cut a cardboard milk carton into a strip about 1½" wide and as long as you can make it. Wrap this strip around the edge of your "cookie," with the waxy side against the cookie. If the strip is not long enough, cut another one and overlap them. Use paper clips greased with petroleum jelly to join the strips. Try to make the top edges level.

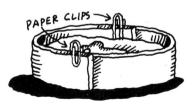

PAPER CLIPS →

1/2 in = 1.27 cm	
1 1/2 in = 3.8 cm	
7 ft = 2.1 m	
2 tsp = 10 ml	

4 Put one cup of water in an empty plastic ice-cream carton. Stir in one cup of plaster of Paris. Stir until it is well mixed and starts to look like cake frosting. Work quickly. Plaster of Paris hardens in a few minutes. **Do not** try to add more water if it is too thick. (You *can* add more plaster.) **Caution: Do not put your hands or fingers in the plaster mix and leave them there "to see what happens"! And do not dump any of the wet plaster down a drain. Leave it in the carton.**

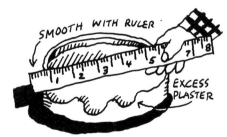

SMOOTH WITH RULER

EXCESS PLASTER

5 Pour your plaster mix on top of the Plasticine. Fill it up to the edge of the cardboard. Use the edge of a ruler or knife to smooth off the top. Wipe off the knife or ruler with a paper towel.

6 Bend a clean (ungreased) paper clip into a loop. Stick the ends of the wire into the wet plaster in your mold. This loop becomes a wall hanger.

7 After a few minutes, the water that may have been on top of the plaster disappears. Use one end of a paper clip to write your name and the date in the drying plaster. Let everything sit for a half hour. Touch the surface of the plaster to see if it has hardened. Carefully unwrap the cardboard strips and lift off the plaster. This is your *negative mold*.

8 Smear the whole bulging side of your negative mold with a *thin* layer of petroleum jelly. Use a small, stiff brush to help work it in and out of the grooves and holes in the "key." Put another greased cardboard collar around your negative mold, waxed side inside. Pour more plaster to make your *positive mold*. Label it and put in a hanger. After an hour, separate your positive and negative molds **carefully!**

9 Two hours after pouring, wash your molds under running water. Use detergent to get rid of any grease. Once the molds are dry, you can paint them any color. Metallic paints like gold or silver look really great!

10 Now go outside and make casts of tracks: footprints of people or other animals, tire-tread marks, whatever looks interesting. When you find a track you would like to cast, clean any

bits of leaves or other junk out of it first. If the soil around the track is crumbly, you can spray the track with hair spray. This will harden and hold little pieces in place. Put a greased cardboard collar around the track and pour in your plaster.
Remember: You can't pre-mix the plaster before you start, so you will have to carry your supplies with you separately.

If you want to make a large cast, bigger than a dinner plate, you will need some reinforcement. Pour in half of your mix and then crisscross several pieces of coat-hanger wire on top of the wet plaster. (Cut the wire with pliers or bend it back and forth until it breaks.) Then pour in the rest of your mix. You might want to leave a loop of wire sticking out for a hanger.

AFTERWORDS

Plaster is made from the mineral *gypsum*. Gypsum looks like rock and is made up of *billions* of crystals. Pieces of gypsum are heated in a fire until about three fourths of the water in the rock evaporates. This breaks down three fourths of the crystals in the gypsum and the rock turns to a powder. When water is added to the powdered rock, presto! The crystals re-form and the powder hardens once again. Instant rock! As the crystals re-form, heat is given off. You can feel this heat while your casts are hardening.

Plaster has been used for about 3,000 years. Our modern product is called plaster of Paris because the soil around Paris in France has much gypsum. Fine-quality plaster has been made in Paris for hundreds of years. But your stuff was probably made in the U.S.A. Where? Check the label.

Police officers often use plaster to make casts — particularly of tire-tread marks and footprints found at the scene of a crime. Then they can bring their outdoor evidence in-

doors, to the courtroom. But folks in the high Rocky Mountains of the Pacific Northwest (Washington and Oregon) have found some curious footprints, too. People have gone into the wild areas and brought back casts of huge footprints. These prints *look* like they were made by humans but are too big to belong to any "normal" man. These are supposed to be prints of prehistoric humans — the Sasquatch, or Bigfoot, of the Rockies.

Some people believe these oversized, human-like creatures exist. Some people even claim to have seen them — describing them as about 7 feet or taller, with long, dark hair all over their bodies. Other people say there is no such thing as Bigfoot. They say it is all a fake and the footprints have been made by someone wearing oversized shoes with soles shaped like feet.

However, since tracks have been found in very wild places, where few people go, whoever is playing the joke is

going through a lot of trouble. And the trick wouldn't be that easy to pull off. Look at your footprints in sand or snow. Now stand on a board bigger than your foot. Where do you sink in the most? You would need to carry a very heavy load to sink the board as far in as your foot alone would sink. And while you were carrying the load, you would have to take strides about twice as long as normal!

Still, if it *is* a hoax, then it has gone on for a long time. There are stories about the capture of a Bigfoot in the Canadian Rockies about 100 years ago. Other countries also have stories and legends about wild humans. The natives of the Himalayan mountains between Nepal and India speak of their "Yeti," or Abominable Snowman. Maybe these creatures exist, maybe they don't. But no one has managed to capture one recently.

What do you think? What will *you* accept as "evidence"? Until you decide, don't go walking in the Rockies alone at night!

FOR MORE INFORMATION . . .

Places to Write and Visit

Here are some places you can write or visit for more information about games, puzzles, and toys. When you write, include your name, address, and age, and be specific about the information you would like to receive. Don't forget to enclose a stamped, self-addressed envelope for a reply.

The Children's Museum
Box 3000
Indianapolis, IN 46206

Omaha Children's Museum
511 S. 18th Street
Omaha, NE 68102

San Francisco International Toy Museum
The Cannery
2801 Leavenworth Street
San Francisco, CA 94133

Toy and Miniature Museum of Kansas City
5235 Oak Street
Kansas City, MO 64112

Further Reading about Games, Puzzles, and Toys

Here are more books you can read about games, puzzles, and toys. Check your local library or bookstore to see if they have the books or can order them for you.

Cat's Cradle, Owl's Eyes. A Book of String Games. Gryski (Morrow Junior Books)
The Famous Name Guessing Game. Barr (Price Stern)
Games From Many Lands. Bernarde (Lion)
Make Your Own Games Workshop. Pearson (Fearon)
Outdoor Games. Alderson (Dufour)
President Games: Puzzles, Quizzes and Mind Teasers for Every George, Abe and Lyndon!
   Swerdlick and Reiter (Price Stern)
The Snark Puzzle Book. Gardner (Prometheus Books)
Toys Around the World and How to Make Them. Fowler (Harcourt)

Hands-On Facts about Games, Puzzles, and Toys

Did you know . . .

- white light, such as sunlight, isn't really white? If broken down into its color components, white light is revealed to be a combination of red, orange, yellow, green, blue, and violet light.

- weather stations, including the U.S. Weather Bureau, once used kites to keep meteorological instruments in the air so that they could register vital information about weather developments?

- plaster is often referred to as "plaster of Paris" because the soil around Paris was once mined to make plaster because of its high gypsum content?

- plaster is often used by law enforcement officers to make molds of evidence like tire-tread marks and footprints at the scene of a crime? This enables them to take valuable evidence into the courtroom that might otherwise be impossible to reproduce.

- until 1876, there were no regulations controlling how much cargo a captain could load onto his ship? Many ships sank, and many lives were lost, because overloaded ships sank easily during storms at sea. Now, ships must have a load-limit line painted on the outside. The line is called the "Plimsoll Line" in honor of the man who instigated the load-limit law.

- saltwater is denser, and therefore heavier, than freshwater?

- a design for a helicopter was drawn up by Italian inventor and artist Leonardo da Vinci almost 500 years before a helicopter was successfully built?

- the expression "you are eating like a bird" for someone who is hardly touching his or her food is misleading? Birds actually eat a great deal. Birds preparing to migrate eat so much before setting out on their journey that they can weigh up to twice their normal weight! This way, they won't have stop so often for snacks along the way.

- the eyesight of hawks and eagles is thought to be ten times better than that of human beings?

- birds purposefully eat grit and gravel? They do this because they have no teeth, and the grit and gravel they stash in their gizzards help them to process and digest their food.

GLOSSARY

atom: a tiny particle of which all things are made. Every atom contains electrons, protons, and neutrons.

biological clock: the natural, internal timing system that seems to be instinctive in most plants and animals.

circadian rhythm: the daily pattern of growth and hormonal activity that is established in most plants and animals.

dispersion: the process of separating the colors of the light spectrum.

electron: a negative particle of electricity that is a part of an atom.

freshwater: water in lakes and streams that does not contain salt.

gizzard: a large, stomach-like part of a bird's digestive system that helps grind up food with the help of grit and pebbles the bird has swallowed.

gypsum: a mineral substance that looks like rock but is made up of billions of crystals.

hormone: a substance produced in certain glands and carried by the bloodstream that regulates growth and some bodily functions, such as reproduction.

internal combustion engine: an engine that burns its own fuel internally.

lift: the phenomenon that results from air flowing over the wings of a plane at a great speed. The wing is designed in such a way that the air pressure above the wing is less than that below the wing, and the difference causes the plane to rise.

mass: the density of a body and how much it weighs.

neutron: a particle of an atom that is neutral (without any electrical charge).

plaster of Paris: a sculpting material made from gypsum which can be molded in liquid form and then dries into a solid.

Plimsoll Line: the line marked on ships to indicate the weight limit point for the ship's cargo.

protons: positive particles of electricity that are a part of atoms.

rods and cones: the cells in the eye that are sensitive to light and color.

"Sasquatch": the Native American name for the legendary "Bigfoot," a part-animal, part-human creature who is thought by some to inhabit the mountains of the Pacific Northwest.

suet: a type of beef fat that is a good food supplement in the winter for birds like woodpeckers that eat insects during the summer.

INDEX